The Best Book on Getting Married

Featuring

The 100 Questions you and your future spouse MUST answer before tying the knot

By

Z. A. Richards

Ari Publishing

Any references to any person living or dead is coincidental

So... You're Getting Married!

I'll start with the most important piece of information regarding marriage that you will ever need to know. And it's that:

EVERY MARRIAGE MAKES ITS <u>OWN</u> RULES

And the goal of this book is for you and your future spouse to set up a list of agreements and compromise guidelines (or rules if you prefer) that you'll both agree to adhere to once married.

Don't listen to what others think your marriage should be or what your supposed duties are or how you should conduct yourself or even who should do what in bed. When it comes to your marriage the only people whose opinion matters is you and your spouse's.

That's it. No one else. Not your parents, or friends or siblings or co-workers, NO ONE. And if you are influenced by what those outside your marriage think or say, you are not ready to be married.

In the old days marriage was simple. Once married, the husband went to work to support the family and the wife stayed home and took care of the house and kids. Husband and wife knew what was expected and tended to their respective responsibilities.

The internet wasn't an issue, porn wasn't an issue, drugs weren't an issue, child daycare wasn't an issue, same-sex marriage wasn't an issue and facebook wasn't an issue. In the past marriage was a one-size fits all.

People stayed married because family, friends and society frowned on divorce. It was thought that divorced people were in some ways defective, that they had failed their partner and subjected their children to a broken home.

But what goes on behind closed doors is often very different than what the public sees.

In today's world there is a new set of rules, a new way of looking at marriage and a new list of things that are expected. Divorce has become common and socially acceptable. However, regardless of what the movies show and television presents as the free-wheeling, post-divorce single life, the reality is that it is often a miserable, and sometimes devastating experience whose effects can last for decades.

So don't agree to marry if you have concerns. Or by telling yourself you can 'always get a divorce' if things go south. That's like jumping out of an airplane with an umbrella, and depending on it to provide you with a safe landing.

And especially don't look at celebrities as examples. They can recover in beautiful tropical locales, go to exclusive parties to meet new people, surround themselves with witty and entertaining friends for weeks and sometimes months if needed.

You'll likely have to go to your 9-5 job the next day.

And that's rough. So I wrote this book to give you and your future spouse the opportunity to see EXACTLY what you're entering into. If you are truly the right person for each other then you two should sail right through this. If not, it's better to know now.

As for my story, I was happily married for 25 years, (dated for 5 years before that) we raised two wonderful children and lived in one of the most beautiful areas of the country. After our children finished college and moved out, I thought the best years of our marriage were ahead of us.

Unfortunately, an overwhelming combination severe personal, physical and financial problems occurring in a very short period of time turned our relationship toxic, which only proves that sometimes, even the best of marriages can't survive.

Following the collapse of my marriage I began researching fellow divorced people and found many similarities in the causes of their breakups. For the middle-aged people like myself, it was usually a combination of age, health and financial issues. However, regarding the younger divorced people, the problem was obvious.

THEY HAD NO IDEA WHO THE OTHER PERSON WAS WHEN THEY MARRIED THEM!

We are a different people than our ancestors with different issues. Many of the problems they had, are no longer valid. And the same goes for the problems today's society brings to the table. I doubt our forbearers even imagined the possibility of Facebook 'Friending" someone they never met.

Marriage is more complex now and we need to learn how to build a marriage that lasts, at least until the kids are grown, and hopefully until you are both laid to rest.

Having done that research I discovered the reasons why many new couple's marriages fell apart. The answers are simple.

- They were so much in love they intentionally ignored the warning signs of their partner's problems.
- They had deep-seated convictions and beliefs they hadn't shared with their partners.
- They kept secrets from their partners regarding important issues (Health, money, genetic disorders etc.)
- They were incompatible sexually.
- They were incompatible morally.

But the main problem? They had convinced themselves that whatever differences or issues they had would, 'go away' after they got married or if they 'loved each other enough'.

If you're reading or listening to this book, keep in mind that attitude will provide you with a life of misery, disappointment and heartbreak. Why? Because in the real world love doesn't conquer all and the person you're marrying (like yourself) has flaws.

Marriage is best served when it is entered into by two people who fully understand the full meaning of the words 'For better or for worse, in sickness and in health, for richer and for poorer and till death do you part.

The problem is that movies, television and romance novels portray normal humans in abnormal terms. We're led to believe that if you try hard enough, you WILL win. That love conquers all; that a solution to any problem will be found. That little Jimmy will get well again and that eventually we will all live happily ever after.

No. That's not realistic.

The entertainment industry knows people want a 'happy ending.' That they want life to be fair and for good things to happen to good people, because that's how they *want* life to be. And we see so many scripted instances of that on television and in movies that we've mistakenly begun to believe that's the way real life works

But it doesn't.

The reality is, life can be hard. Things can get tough, very tough. And as much as you love your spouse, you will be tempted. You WILL be tested. Money will get tight. One of you may become seriously ill or develop an emotional disorder or be permanently injured in an accident. You might lose everything in a natural disaster or an economic meltdown. A child may die.

And it's very possible your dreams may never come true, because in most cases, they don't.

But if you are married to someone who truly loves you and one whom you truly love, then you can survive life's difficulties, and by working together, you can weather almost any storm and grow even closer.

How can you be sure you've found that person and can count on them through tough times? You find out by you and your future spouse taking this questionnaire and answering the 100 questions that follow.

Set aside a couple of hours in a place where the two of you can be alone and talk frankly. By the time all the questions are answered there will very likely be some emotional upheaval. You will learn things about your potential mate that you never knew and likely never suspected.

This is not to say that once you learn your partner's shortcomings, your relationship is doomed. Quite the opposite, it simply gives you both the opportunity to face those issues and solve them or accept the reality that they are deal-breakers that cannot be overcome.

And be completely honest! If you think these questions are hard to truthfully answer now, consider your future devastated child asking 'Why can't daddy live with us anymore?' or saying things like 'Mommy, please don't leave me.'

So make a pact with your soon-to-be spouse to answer every question truthfully. If it helps, make believe you and your future mate are tied up and hooked up to a lie detector, and there is a man with a gun standing behind you both with orders to shoot the first one who fails to be completely honest.

A little gruesome, true, but down the road you'll be glad you came clean.

No one is perfect. We all have annoying flaws and weird rituals that we must adjust to if we want to live together. He can learn to scrape his plate and put it in the dishwasher after eating, to tuck his shoes under the bed so no one trips over them and she can remember never to bring fish into the house because he's highly allergic.

But insisting our kids be raised as atheists? Depending on who you are, that might be a deal-breaker.

Here's something to always keep in mind. The two biggest reasons for the collapse of a marriage is infidelity and resentment.

Infidelity is big and right there in your face to either deal with or break up.

Resentment is sneaky and insidious. It builds over time when one partner doesn't carry their share of the load, fails to take their partners concerns seriously or lies, thinking the partner isn't clever enough to see the dishonesty.

Infidelity often cripples a marriage.

Resentment kills it.

So, have you found a quiet place where you can talk undisturbed for an extended period? Ready to tell the truth the whole truth and nothing but the truth so help you God? (Or whatever deity, or lack thereof, you subscribe to.)

If you're reading this as an e book or listening to an audio book you will need a notebook and pen (or you can type the questions and your answers on your electronic device as you will likely want to refer to them years later when a sticky problem rears its head.) The questions are for you both. Write down each answer and initial at the bottom. In the instances where you disagree, write out the compromise or alternative and then initial.

What you're about to do is form an agreement that states what your behavior will be once you are married. Take it as seriously as you would when signing any legal and binding contract and perhaps even more so because most legal and binding contract last for only a specific period of time.

This contract is until death.

Okay my friends, let's get started.

The questions are broken into three categories: HOME, FAMILY and RELATIONSHIP. Think carefully before answering. Any question you don't seriously consider now, may come back to haunt you later.

HOME

1) Do you both want children? If so, how many?

Write your answer here:

Point(s) to consider: This simple question has caused more marriage trouble than one would expect. Primarily because one partner mistakenly believed that the other, over time, would have a change of heart.

If a baby is brought into the mix especially if one of the partners specifically said they didn't want children, there will be trouble. DON'T ASSUME your partner will fall in love with the child once it's born. More likely the child will be resented and ignored, resulting in emotional problems for the child and he or she will be a constant source of derision between the two of you. Don't have a child or agree to have one to satisfy your partner. If you feel strongly about your position, it's better to find out now than later, when much more is invested in the relationship

2) What religion, if any, will the children be raised in?

Write your answer here:

Point(s) to consider: The best way to resolve this question is to raise the children in the religion of the parent most willing to take them to services at their house of worship. Don't insist your child be raised in your religion if you aren't willing to immerse yourself in the faith and set an example for the child by following its teachings.

3) Who will handle the money? Pay the bills?

Write your answer here:

Point(s) to consider: Don't let your ego involve itself in this. Whichever is better at handling money and following a budget should be the one in charge. Word to the wise, if both of you are contributing income, it is likely one of you will eventually want something not in the budget (he wants a big screen TV, she wants the latest cell-phone.) Factor this in to avoid resentment. Nobody likes being told what they can and cannot do with their own money

4) Will the money be in individual accounts or a joint account?

Write your answer here:

Point(s) to consider: Best way to handle this is to have two joint accounts. The checking account should be John and/or Jane Smith. This way either one of you can withdrawn money for monthly bills and expenses as they accrue. The joint savings account should be John AND Jane Smith and set so money can only be withdrawn when both spouses are present.

This prevents either of the partners from withdrawing funds from the savings account without the knowledge or consent of the other.

5) What is the breakdown of responsibilities regarding house repair? (Is he responsible for the outside and she for the inside or what combination?)

Write your answer here:

Point(s) to consider: This isn't as simple a question as you might think. Again, the answer is whoever is most able. I'm friends with a couple where he does the vacuuming and laundry and gardening and she does the physical house repairs like replacing water hoses, fixing loose roof shingles and unclogging the toilet.

6) Who does the laundry?

Write your answer here:

Point(s) to consider: If it's only the two of you and you have a washing machine and dryer, it is suggested you do your own laundry. If he/she has a full time job, he/she doesn't need any extra chores especially those he/she can do him/herself.

7) Who does the cooking?

Write your answer here:

Point(s) to consider: Whoever is better at it and enjoys doing it. BUT, the cook doesn't do clean up. So after the meal is enjoyed it's time for the other partner to step up and clean the mess.

8) Who takes out the garbage?

Write your answer here:

Point(s) to consider: The garbage like other daily chores should be divvied up equally. Make sure the distribution of chores is fair. Resentment builds when one partner feels they're doing more than their fair share.

9) Who cleans the bathroom?

Write your answer here:

Point(s) to consider: Traditionally the wife cleaned the house however, with most women working outside the home and putting in as many hours as their spouses that's no longer a given. So again maintenance chores need to be evenly distributed, especially when it's usually the man whose aim is the problem with the toilet and whose hair is usually what's clogging the bathtub drain.

10) Do you want to have a pet(s)?

Write your answer here:

Point(s) to consider: Be very careful here. Pets are a big responsibility. They live for decades, sometimes destroy personal items (shoes and gloves) household furniture (chairs and couches) knock over and eat out of the garbage and urinate and defecate inside the house so make sure you agree as to who cleans up after that happens.

11) If a dog, who will walk him?

Write your answer here:

Point(s) to consider: A dog often has to go 3 to four times a day. Older dogs even more and should you live in a cold climate, night walks can be brutal. Plus most towns and cities have laws requiring you to pick up their poop and properly dispose of it. So should you decide to have one, make sure you both agree on whose responsible for walking him.

12) If a cat, who will change the litter box?

Write your answer here:

Point(s) to consider: Even with today's technology, cat boxes, if unattended, smell terrible and their odor can seep into your drapes and upholstery. They also need to sharpen their claws and will do so on the furniture if not trained otherwise. It's a big responsibility so make sure you're both agree on whose handles it and how often.

13) Will guns be kept in the house? If so, where and with what type of locks?

Write your answer here:

Point(s) to consider: Give this one a lot of thought. Are either of you quick to anger? Because spousal homicides are far more likely if there are guns in the house. On the other hand, if you are both even tempered and you live in a rural area and don't have easy access to police protection you will likely need at least one firearm. This issue is often a deal-breaker so make sure you're both in agreement and are properly trained in firearm usage should you decide that having one is necessary.

14) Will you both attend religious services?

Write your answer here:

Point(s) to consider: There is an old saying. *The family that prays together stays together* and studies have shown that couples that attend weekly services have fewer divorces. However, this is a personal matter. Regardless if you do or don't attend, do not attempt to guilt your partner into either coming with you or staying home with you.

15) If you have children, will both of you bring them to services?

Write your answer here:

Point(s) to consider: Whether you and your spouse attend religious services is something you'll have to decide for yourselves and your children. In my opinion (and this is only my opinion) I think a child should have religious instruction until age eighteen. They will of course, battle you on this as they get older (mine certainly did, but now take their own children to services) I believe a sturdy religious education with a strong emphasis on right and wrong will help keep the child on the straight and narrow during their very difficult teen years.

Still you're the parents and it's your decision.

16) How important are sports? If very, do you agree on the amount of time that will be spent watching them?

Write your answer here:

Point(s) to consider: Some people are sports fanatics. Mostly men and often women turn this into an issue when it doesn't have to be. During the time you spent dating you must have come to realize the extent of his obsession with sports. Like many things THIS WILL NOT CHANGE ONCE YOU GET MARRIED. And don't try to force the issue by parading around in skimpy lingerie during the big game and then getting angry when he asks you to get out of the way of the TV. Before you get married sit down and talk about this and come to a compromise about how often sports will be watched in your home. Don't put this off. Sport addiction like alcoholism and chronic gambling are often deal-breakers.

17) Do either of you do drugs? If so, will they be done inside the house?

Write your answer here:

Point(s) to consider: Either of you smoking an occasional joint will likely

NOT be a deal-breaker however, now that you are becoming a family, do you still want to meet some shady guy on a street corner to buy a bag of weed? Or does your recreational use include some stronger and potentially dangerous drugs like steroids, cocaine, LSD or prescription meds? Those type of drugs change your personality and often not for the better. Drug use is often a deal breaker. You both should be VERY straightforward regarding your position on this.

18) If you do drugs will they be kept inside the house?

Write your answer here:

Point(s) to consider: This can be a real stickler as time goes by. One partner might not mind at first but after a while the constant possibility they might be discovered by someone they don't want finding them becomes a problem. Plus there is always the possibility that after a falling out with a neighbor you may be ratted out to the police.

19) Will you continue to use drugs after you have children?

Write your answer here:

Point(s) to consider: Again, this is a difficult topic. Being high in front of your children is a lousy way to parent. Drugs affect your mood, clouds your judgment and sets an exceedingly poor example. Yet some people can barely get through the day without some sort of mood enhancement. So discuss how this will be handled now if it is an issue

20) Alcohol consumption, who drinks what and when?

Write your answer here:

Point(s) to consider: If neither are drinkers then there is no problem. If you do, then this question needs to be taken very seriously. The reason is some people can drink as much as they want and the only ill effect is they fall asleep.

Others however, undergo a frightening personality change, turning a usually easy going, friendly person into a belligerent bully looking to start an argument or fight.

If this describes your partner after too many drinks he/she has a Jekyll and Hyde personality and it's not something that's going to go away. It affects women as much as it does men and this might be a deal-breaker if your future spouse has a taste for alcohol.

Regardless of gender no one wants to be in a marriage with someone with those tendencies. And if you're not sure if they are that type, get them drunk and find out. Better to know now what you are entering into than later when it's too late.

21) How many and what type of vehicles do you want?

Write your answer here:

Point(s) to consider: How much to spend on a car or truck sometimes presents a real problem when both partners have a distinctly different view.

One may look at a vehicle as merely a mode of transportation and would be happy with a stripped down economy car, while the other views their ride as an extension of their personality, meaning only the best will do. Now is the time to sort that out.

22) Who will drive when you're going out together?

Write your answer here:

Point(s) to consider: With most couples it's usually the husband. It's been a social convention since the advent of the car but new factors are changing that and it's something that needs to be agreed upon.

A married couple I know ran into that exact difficulty. She is a high powered executive and owns an expensive luxury car. He's is a building contractor and owns a big powerful pickup truck. They both enjoy dining at top restaurants.

The problem is, she doesn't want to climb out of a giant truck in an evening gown, and he feels that if they're going to take her car, then he should drive because he's the man and so refuses to go to a valet parking restaurant if she's behind the wheel.

23) Are you a conservative or a liberal?

Write your answer here:

Point(s) to consider: This often becomes an issue and it doesn't need to be. Unless one of you is personally involved in politics, neither of you can do anything to change the system so your opinions on this or that topic are meaningless. However, those with extremely opposite views are likely to have different ideologies on other topics so it's important you know where your potential mate stands on issues that may involve you both such as abortion, gun control and healthcare.

24) Vegetarian or carnivore?

Write your answer here:

Point(s) to consider: This is rarely a deal-breaker if one's a meat eater and the other is not, but making separate meals in separate pots and pans can grow annoying. Plus, like religion there has to be a discussion on how the children will be raised. Now is the time to have that discussion.

25) Early Bird or Night Owl?

Write your answer here:

Point(s) to consider: This can be a bigger problem than you realize. Having a spouse who is just revving up when you're ready to call it a night or one who can barely climb out of bed when you're getting ready for a sunrise jog, can wear thin and lead to problems. If this is going to be an issue you should figure out how to handle it now and not wait until it causes real problems after you're married.

26) Going to restaurants/concerts/clubs?

If so, how often? Alone or together?
Write your answer here:

Point(s) to consider: Once people get married they encounter a period of adjustment. The dating years are over and building a life and family together become more important. In some cases however, one of the partners isn't ready to give up the flashy restaurants, music concerts and night clubs. All of which are expensive. So now is the time to work out how much time and money will be set aside for that type of entertainment.

27) Socializing with neighbors-Barbequing/dinner parties?

If so, how often?
Write your answer here:

Point(s) to consider: Some couples love socializing with the neighbors, having barbeques and dinner parties. Others prefer to keep to themselves and are uncomfortable at social events. If you're both the same type you're in luck, if not, there is going to be problems if not worked out now, because however it turns out one of the partners is going to feel put upon and resent it.

28) Do you have credit card debt, or outstanding student loans?

Will you pay it off together or individually?
Write your answer here:

Point(s) to consider: Address this topic now, make a plan and stick to it until the financial obligations are resolved. This is a ticking time bomb especially if one partner is debt free and the other has excessive outstanding bills. The partner with debt will be unable to contribute their fare share into the family account because their paycheck is paying down the debt, while the other is forced to pick up the slack. This often leads to resentment so if this is an issue, you need to address it now.

29) Have you or your spouse ever filed for bankruptcy, if so when?

Write your answer here:

Point(s) to consider: Depending on where you live, bankruptcies can remain on your credit reports for a considerable period of time. It will affect your purchasing power and may prevent you from having a credit card, which will present a problem when you want to rent cars or reserve hotel rooms.

Certain debt cannot be removed by bankruptcy filings such as tax debt and student loans. Make sure your future spouse is fully aware of your credit status and how your outstanding debts were settled.

30) Do you intend to buy a house or rent?

Write your answer here:

Point(s) to consider: Give this some thought and first decide if either of you is handy and capable of doing repairs. (Doesn't matter which one) A house is usually a good investment and often used to provide retirement income. However, over a 30 year mortgage that house will require extensive repairs and upkeep. Will either of you have the time to do repairs following a week at work? How much assistance will your mate provide? Remember the days of the husband doing repair chores on his days off went out with the fedora hat. Today's marriage is a 50/50 relationship and the harder both partners work to keep it that way the longer it will last.

31) How important are material possessions?

Write your answer here:

Point(s) to consider: This can be a trick question. What it boils down to is whether either one, or both of you, highly value material possessions. I was dating a woman for a while and we got along well until we had a discussion on what we envisioned our future house would look like. I was a musician at the time and saw myself in a spacious Greenwich Village loft sparsely furnished with only the bare essentials. (I hate clutter or having to go look for something. I like simple and functional)

She envisioned a suburban house filled with finely crafted furniture, elaborate paintings, expensive china, crystal chandeliers, marble tiled floors and imported rugs.

I couldn't see myself living in such a house and she couldn't see herself living in mine.

The relationship ended soon after that.

32) **Do you respect your spouse's possessions?**

What if you don't like them? What if they are hideous? (For example: the ladies leg lamp in *A Christmas Story*) **Write your answer here**:

Point(s) to consider: Respect is important in a relationship. Not valuing someone possessions can lead to resentment. Too often people make the mistake of thinking that if something isn't important or valuable to them, how important can it be to someone else? The answer, VERY. Once again TV shows and movies portray the wife throwing out a husband's old football jersey or whatever and the situation is made light of. It's not and can lead to serious problems in the marriage.

Most women take the lead when it comes to home furnishings and clothing and most men are fine with that. However, there are boundaries regarding each partner's possessions that need to be respected regardless of how you feel about them.

33) Should the last one using something until it's finished, (toilet paper, empty milk carton etc) be responsible to replace it.

Write your answer here:

Point(s) to consider: You would be surprised at how much trouble this causes, and often rightly so, especially when it comes to toilet paper. However you just might have to adapt to this if your partner is someone easily distracted or normally forgetful. You can't turn a duck into a giraffe.

34) In what style will your home be decorated and who will make the buying decisions?

Write your answer here:

Point(s) to consider: Usually it's the wife who decides how the house is furnished, what color the walls are painted and whether there will be carpeted or hardwood floors.

But as in all things, your spouse's opinion is far more important than what your friends and relatives think, and he may have surprisingly strong opinions about what he wants or doesn't want in your home.

It will be the two of you living there and both must be comfortable with their surroundings.

Compromise. Remember you're a team.

If she doesn't want that moose head on the wall then leave it off. If he doesn't want your only bathroom done up in pink with frills and lace and potpourri, then tone it down to something he can live with.

You can likely expect he'll want a big screen TV and a comfortable recliner in the living room. That's usually non-negotiable with most guys. Other than that in most cases, she usually can set it up how she pleases.

35) What type and size bed do you want?

Write you answer here:

Point(s) to consider: You will spend one-third of your life in bed and so it's very important that you buy one you're both comfortable in. This might be more challenging than you think especially if she likes a hard mattress and he likes it soft. One partner may want the bed small and intimate and the other big and spacious.

Some prefer waterbeds and some hate them. Same goes for those space age foam mattress that many love to sleep on but find it uncomfortable when making love.

This purchase will more important than nearly anything else you will buy so make sure the bed is both comfortable and provides a good night's sleep.

Family

36) Have you met your future in-laws?

Write you answer here:

Point(s) to consider: If you haven't, you probably should. The people who raised you future spouse can tell you a lot about who they are. (I'm sure you've heard the old saying: 'The apple doesn't fall far from the tree.')

See how close they are as a family. If they aren't, your partner might have difficulties forming a close bond with you and the children. In the future that may be something you'll have to help them with.

37) Is he a Momma's boy? She a Daddy's girl?

Write your answer here:

Point(s) to consider: Other than your partner receiving specialized training from a licensed psychologist you won't likely change this. In many cases it can be harmless although annoying BUT, there is real danger if you and that particular parent have a falling out. Your spouse will likely take their side. So if you want to keep peace, *and* the relationship with your spouse is otherwise healthy, then do whatever is necessary to keep a good relationship with that parent.

38) Does your future spouse have 'Mommy/Daddy issues?

Write your answer here:

Point(s) to consider: This is the dark side of 'Momma's boy' and 'Daddy's girl'. It's a serious emotional issue and one likely to require professional help. Studies have shown that many people, when looking for a mate, gravitate toward people with personalities similar to that of one of their parents.

Problems occur when there are serious unresolved issues between parent and child and they— because of your similarities to that parent—start transposing those problems onto you. This disorder can grow stronger if you happen to physically resemble that parent.

If there is to be any chance of that relationship working out, that partner must undergo therapy to resolve those issues or you will likely find yourself married to someone determined to make you pay for their parent's mistreatment.

39) Will you be taking your spouses' last name or some configuration thereof?

Write your answer here:

Point(s) to consider: Women used to automatically take their husbands name. Now it's a matter for discussion. Some couples do a combo package. For example: Karen Miller-Jones or Tiffany Simms-Anderson. Keep in mind any children you have will have to carry this lengthy surname around for the rest of their lives so, kick it around, make a decision and stick with it. Friends and family will likely go along with a onetime name change after marriage but will grow annoyed with any future adjustments.

40) How often will in-laws visit?

Write your answer here:

Point(s) to consider: Set the ground rules on in-law visits NOW. Nothing harms new marriages as much as interference from in-laws. Remember the two of you are building a life-long relationship and putting together your marriage's 'Marriage Rules'. There will be considerable trial and error and the last thing you'll need is an in-law's input on how you're doing.

Everyone will want to give you advice from their experience BUT, since every marriage has its own rules of behavior, most of it won't apply.

Set a limit on the number of time the in-laws can drop by and insist (but nicely) that they abide by them.

41) How often will you visit them?

Write you answer here:

Point(s) to consider: Remember you'll need time to adjust to this new situation and spending a lot of time with the folks will only stall the formation of your own independent family. Even if you have lived together before marriage, once married the trial period is over. From that day on and for the rest of both your lives, in all things, remember, YOUR SPOUSE COMES FIRST.

42) If from different religions, which holiday celebrations will you both attend and at what family's home?

Write your answer here:

Point(s) to consider: Now would be a good time to discuss how that will play out. Some couples attend both holiday celebrations because the grandparents want to see the kids and if you go to one house and not the other, people get slighted and problems arise. The best way is for you and your spouse to set a schedule of who will see who when and where and give a copy of that schedule to both families and try to make the best of it.

43) Do you allow a parent to criticize your spouse?

Write your answer here:

Point(s) to consider: There are few instances as volatile as this one. Any time a parent criticizes their child (your spouse) you're going to want to defend them, and when you do, your in-law's spouse steps in to defend *them* and then your spouse may tell you to mind your own business and all hell breaks loose.

On the other hand if you stay out of it, your spouse may be angry with you for not coming to their defense.

So, create a plan to deal with this so you'll both know how to react should this situation arise.

Then <u>stick to it.</u>

If your spouse says to never interfere, then never interfere. If your spouse says the gloves are off, then the gloves are off and whatever happens to your relationship to them, happens. The important part is that it doesn't affect YOUR relationship with each other.

44) Do you allow a parent to criticize how your home is kept?

Write your answer here:

Point(s) to consider: Again, volatile. Remember your spouse and in-laws have a completely different skill set when it comes to relating to each other. However, it is always advisable to take your spouse's side.

If a parent criticizes how your house is kept, you both respond "We like it that way!" and if that doesn't put an end to it then say something like. "I find it interesting that you would never enter a neighbor's house, someone you barely know and criticize their home, yet you feel perfectly comfortable to come here and criticize mine, and I'm someone you supposedly love."

That will likely put the brakes on further critiques.

45) Do you allow your parents to criticize your methods of disciplining your children?

Write your answer here:

Point(s) to consider: Absolutely not, unless of course, *you're* <u>not</u> disciplining them. Remember, the grandparents love your kids probably as much as you do and want them to become well-mannered, responsible adults. This behavior needs to be taught when they are young.

There are few things more aggravating than a being subjected to the bellowing and misbehaving of a small child, especially when the parent is doing nothing to make that behavior stop.

After having children quickly establish yourself as the boss. Remember you are their parent not their friend and they must learn to follow your directives to the letter if for no other reason than for their own safety. If you want your children to be expressive free spirits, that's fine, in the privacy of your own home. But don't subject others to their tantrums and bad behavior. And if a parent points out a problem with your parenting skills, and your kids are unruly, then perhaps you need to listen.

46) If the kids are unruly do you spank them? If so, who does the spanking?

Write your answer here:

Point(s) to consider: In all the years my two kids lived with us I only spanked them once. We were blessed with very good children and usually a stern vocal reprimand would be enough to put an end to bad behavior. In each case where the misbehavior was enough to require a spanking, my wife and I decided I'd be the one to administer the punishment.

Both times it broke my heart but it had to be done. In both instances the child did something they knew was wrong, knew their action would deeply upset the person they did it to and did it anyway.

My grown children joke about it now. Me? I recall the old cartoons where a parent was preparing to spank a child and say, "This is going to hurt me more than it does you."

Never believed it as a kid.

I believe it now.

47) Are there any genetic defects in your future spouses' family? Mental illness, suicides, pedophilia, phobias, Down syndrome, bipolar, diabetes, congenital heart disease, high rate of breast cancer etc.

Write your answer here:

Point(s) to consider: It's only fair that your future mate be aware of any potential health problems that might pop up during the course of your marriage. It is also only fair to note that the problems you'll encounter during your marriage will probably have nothing to do with the genetic history. In many ways life is a crap shoot, still, forewarned is forearmed.

48) Allergies or Asthma?

Write your answer here:

Point(s) to consider: Because most people have allergies in one form or another they are often overlooked as a health concern. However some allergies can have serious and dangerous reactions (peanuts, penicillin.) And because Asthma is generally regulated with an inhaler, this too is often overlooked. Be aware of what to look for and what action to take should your children start showing indications that they may have one of these conditions.

49) If your spouse is a professional, will he/she be expected to give free advice or services to members of the family? (Car mechanic, doctor, lawyer)

Write your answer here:

Point(s) to consider: As much as you or your spouse may not like it, relatives coming to you for your professional expertise may be unavoidable without causing hurt feelings and family discord.

But it is important that your in-laws know the extent of your expertise and understand that you don't exceed those boundaries. Make it clear you won't give advice on cancer if you are a cardiologist and refuse to diagnose what is wrong with your brother-in-laws motorcycle if you are a car mechanic.

50) Will you agree to host relatives in your home during their vacation if you live in a resort area?

Write your answer here:

Point(s) to consider: This is another of those petty annoyances that often pop up during a marriage and again one that must be firmly addressed. I live in a popular resort town and for years members of me and my ex's family came to regard our home as their yearly free vacation destination.

It may have been a vacation for them but to us it was a yearly inconvenience. We still had jobs and daily chores to tend to. Finally we sold the big house and moved to a smaller place that couldn't accommodate guests. We soon discovered we weren't as popular as they led us to believe once they had to shell out money for motels and restaurants.

51) Will you or spouse be expected to help elderly parents with health, home maintenance or upkeep?

Write you answer here:

Point(s) to consider: You might think this is a long way off and in most cases it likely is. However sooner or later you are going to have to deal with it. Parents get old, health issues crop up and prevent them from doing certain chores like mowing the lawn and washing the windows. Nursing home care is expensive, as are daily care-givers.

Discuss this with your partner and create a list of options.

52) Will you or your spouse be expected to take in a widowed parent when they can no longer live alone?

Write your answer here:

Point(s) to consider: Few things can upset a marriage as much as adding a new member, especially one who is accustomed to making the rules and having them carried out.

A friend once informed me that "Any house a parent moves into becomes *their* house."

This is a big adjustment and often a cause of resentment by the other partner and understandingly so. So before that possibility presents itself, discuss your options and possible solutions.

53) Will you or your spouse be expected to babysit your relative's kids while they 'run a few errands?'

Write your answer here:

Point(s) to consider: If you live near your relatives it is almost inevitable. And this may not be a bad thing. Raising kids takes a lot of work and having a built in family 'tag team' may take some of the pressure off but once again, make sure the rules are firmly established before this becomes a regular *'thing'*

And don't be concerned about whether your spouses' family or your own relatives 'like you' for being Johnny or Janey on-the-spot. The first of the Marriage Rules should be 'Your spouse comes first". So the moment *their* kids becomes *your* problem, make it clear your services won't be available until conditions change.

54) Does any member of the family have a prison record?

Write your answer here:

Point(s) to consider: While it's true every family is allowed its secrets, you are about to enter into that family and need to have full disclosure as to what you're getting into, especially if it's something serious like a close family member having been convicted of pedophilia or manslaughter. Even more important if on occasion that family member is in close contact with your child.

55) Were you sexually molested as a child? If so, by whom?

Write your answer here:

Point(s) to consider: Children are NEVER responsible for the sex acts they performed or had performed on them by a predator family member or family friend. If you were a victim, tell your soon to be spouse what happened and who was responsible.

You want to make absolutely sure none of your children are in a situation where they can be sexually molested by the same predator.

56) Does your future mate have a DUI or DWI conviction?

Write your answer here:

Point(s) to consider: This can affect you. Once married it can raise YOUR insurance premiums and should they be convicted a second time within a ten year period, they can go to jail.

Imagine being a new parent and having your spouse incarcerated. And don't assume this is only a problem for men, DUI and DWI convictions for women have been steadily rising for years as well as the number of incarcerations.

57) Will you always take your spouse's side when they're in an argument even if you know your spouse is wrong?

Write your answer here:

Point(s) to consider: The issue here is not what the difference of opinion is between your future spouse and their opponent, because no one will remember that. What will be remembered is whose side you took. Especially if family is involved.

Admittedly it is a difficult choice.

However, since you are about to leave your family and start a new one with your partner, then your loyalty needs to shift to the person you're about to spend the rest of your life with.

And yes, you may be an independent person with the right to your own opinions but this is neither the time nor place for it. Your future spouse needs to know if you have their back in any future confrontations.

Neither side wants or cares for your sage advice, wise council, or problem solving skills. This is about loyalty and if you don't take your future spouses' side here—regardless of how stupid their argument—your rock-solid marriage will have a serious crack in it before it even begins.

58) Do you apologize for a relative's errant behavior instead of holding them responsible for their actions?

Write your answer here:

Point(s) to consider: Most families have at least one. The uncle who gets drunk then lets everybody know what he really thinks of them, or the sister who says whatever stupid thing comes into her head regardless of how hurtful or rude. Many families attempt to blow it off with a 'Well, that's just how Uncle Billy gets when he gets a few drinks in him or don't mind Sister Sara, words just fly out her mouth before she can stop them.'

Nonsense. Although people tend to try and avoid confrontation sometimes Uncle Billy and Sister Sara need to be brought up short and told their remarks are cruel, hurtful and inconsiderate and that's no way to treat the people they supposedly love.

That may put an end to the behavior and it might not, but everyone will understand why you and your spouse keep your distance from Uncle Billy and Sister Sara. Plus you two may be described to the rest of the family as the ones who won't abide fools.

59) Have you ever compromised your values and dated people you shouldn't have to avoid being alone or to make someone else happy?

Write your answer here:

Point(s) to consider: Parents and family members often put a lot of pressure on their unmarried adult members to tie the knot and it's not always because they want to see them happily married, but because they don't want other members of the family to view their adult children as odd or unmarryable.

These young adults often feel the pressure and go out with people they normally wouldn't just to avoid being alone or being thought of as undateable.

I saw a bumper sticker once that read, 'Better to have loved and lost than to remain married to a psycho.'

Ask anyone who has been through it and they'll tell you although loneness is unpleasant, being married to someone you don't love or who makes your life miserable is far, far worse.

Word to the wise. Never, ever marry someone to please anyone other than yourself. That person may be disappointed or heartbroken by your refusal but you should never take on a life of misery and unhappiness just to make that someone else happy.

NEVER.

60) Taking care of a relative's pets. Who will be responsible?

Write your answer here:

Point(s) to consider: Every so often one of your relatives or in-laws will need to leave town and will ask you to take care of their animals or pets while they're gone. This is usually a minor inconvenience and should be done in the spirit of family as they would be expected to do the same for you.

However, for some reason you personally can't do it, **DO NOT OFFER THE SERVICES OF YOUR PARTNER WITHOUT CONSULTING THEM FIRST!**

Remember you are their future spouse not their boss or supervisor and doing this will unknowingly likely build a fire of resentment that will take a long time to put out.

61) List the behaviors allowed by your family but not allowed by your spouse's family. Make sure the lists match.

Write your answer here:

Point(s) to consider: For example: Does your future spouse's family allow any visitor to help themselves from the refrigerator or cupboards? Does your own family expect all visitors to request what they want from the host or hostess? Does your future spouse's family request visitors take off their shoes or boots and leave them on the mud porch. Does your family make no such request? Does your future spouse's family allow the dog to beg for food while you're at the dinner table? Does yours strictly forbid it?

Many of the behaviors you and your future spouse were brought up with will likely continue after you're married unless you agree to what changes should be made now.

Let your future spouse know now that you won't tolerate having your dinner interrupted by the family dog pawing at you while you're trying to eat or permit visitors with mud covered shoes or boots to track dirt onto your carpets.

62) You've been offered a high-paying job in a different state, do you accept?

Write your answer here:

Point(s) to consider: There is a lot to consider here. First, your spouse may already have a high paying job here and there's no guarantee there will be a similar one at the new location and therefore not want to move. Second, you likely don't have any friends or relatives there, so who do you go to when you need help? How will your spouse feel about being uprooted and moved away from their family and friends? What if that new job doesn't work out?

Whatever choice you both decide upon, <u>stick with it.</u> No regrets no 'what if's' and absolutely no recriminations. Peoples' lives turn out depend largely on the opportunities they're given. A lot of coverage is given to the big risks and big payoffs, but remember, they are in the minority. So if the decision you both made doesn't pan out, or clearly becomes the best thing you ever did, that's life. Count your blessings, or lick your wounds but in any case, get right back into the game.

63) Your spouse's new job requires long hours and frequent business trips, will that be a problem?

Write your answer here:

Point(s) to consider: To acquire the life you want for tomorrow, you have to put in the time today. That's a fact of life. Financial security takes a lot of hard work. The question is how much is too much? Absence may make the heart grow fonder but too much absence leads to resentment and feelings of abandonment.

Discuss this with your partner and be blunt about what your needs are. If financial security is your primary concern, then accept your partner's absence as the sacrifice necessary to achieve that goal.

If that amount of time away from home is unacceptable, then make that clear and come to terms with the fact that your retirement years will be spent frugally and with few extravagances.

Relationship

It can get intense here. Still remember to answer honestly.

64) Just how well do you know him or her?

Write your answer here:

Point(s) to consider: Of all the questions in this book, this is the most important. Why? Because my rescarch has shown the majority of short term marriages ended because one partner had no idea what the other partner was really like. Or even worse, was convinced they could change that person, or even worse than that, they refused to acknowledge their partner's fatal flaws.

You cannot change someone.
That only happens in books and movies or where there is long term psychological counseling and retraining.

Why? Because a person's personality is developed over a period of decades. It is the skill set they use to deal with daily life. They are not going to change regardless of how much they care for you. Oh, they may attempt to and may succeed for a short period of time but as the old saying goes, 'A leopard cannot change its spots'. So make the effort to really know your future mate before tying the knot

If he's a 'bad boy' prone to violence, you will likely be a battered wife. If she's a flirt and an attention whore, you will likely be cheated on. As an adult, certain realities must be acknowledged, accepted and dealt with. Remember short term heartbreak is better than life-long misery.

65) **Prenup?**

Write your answer here:

Point(s) to consider: I can almost hear you both saying, "I wish one of us had enough money to make a prenuptial agreement an issue but we're just starting out."

Understood, but in some cases one of the partners has money and so the matter needs to be addressed. From a moral standpoint one should only get to keep what one earns and with present day's society's belief of equality in all things, one shouldn't be automatically entitled to lifelong financial support simply by marrying someone.

Money matters cause a lot of trouble so make sure both parties agree on the financials before entering into a commitment that if it ends, will only make the divorce lawyers rich.

66) **How different is your financial upbringing?**

Write your answer here:

Point(s) to consider: How many fairy tales have the poor, sweet and kindhearted girl marrying the rich handsome prince and they live happily ever after?

In reality, a considerable distance between the two families' finances during their childhood years can be a problem when it comes to the way they view money.

If one partner grew up in a wealthy family with no money concerns, it's likely he/she will spend freely and sometimes frivolously. The other partner, coming from meager beginnings, will likely pinch every penny to avoid ever having to return to a life of scrimping and saving.

He/She might view the lavish expenditures, (even if they're on them) as wasteful and the other partner may see the lack of appreciation as being miserly and judgmental. Talk about how you view money, savings and finances. Make sure you have similar views on how and where it should be spent.

67) **What do you expect from your partner, is it more than they're capable of giving?**

Write you answer here:

Point(s) to consider: This is another instance where movies, TV and romance novels muddy the waters and lead to problems in marriages. Women swoon when the hero sweeps the female lead off her feet and carries her off to his yacht or castle. Men are in constant search of that sweet faced Pollyanna whose only joy and interest in life is to make him happy.

And both feel cheated when they discover their spouse will never be the person of their dreams. If you are a woman in love with a kind, loving introverted nerd, don't be disappointed if he doesn't wade into battle when some bulky biker whistles at you.

And if you're a man, and in love with a smart, witty professional women, don't expect her to follow you around like a puppy and hang on your every word.

If you're mature enough to be married then the time has come to accept the realities of life. First, that your childhood fantasies were just fantasies, and second, that your dream spouse was just a dream.

68) Do you respect your partner's judgment?

Write your answer here:

Point(s) to consider: This is very
important. There is a very good
chance that an emergency will occur
somewhere in your married life and
you will have to depend on your
spouse's decisions to protect you
and your family.

How does he/she react to serious
situations? Are they clear headed
and responsible or do they become
panicky and scattered-brained?
Somewhere down the road your very
life may depend on their ability to
function.

Be sure they can.

69) **Do you have a temper?**

Write your answer here:

Point(s) to consider: Having a temper is not necessarily a bad thing. It allows you to stand up for your rights and make sure you're respected and treated fairly. However an uncontrollable temper is a serious disorder and one not to be taken lightly. Jails are filled with people who flew off the handle and committed horrific acts of violence in moments of blinding rage.

If you future spouse is someone who cannot control their temper for whatever reason, they need anger management counseling to learn the skills necessary to keep their temper under control.

If they won't do it, refuse to marry them until they do. Rageaholics seriously hurt people and usually those closest to them.

70) Do you use sex or withholding affection as a method to get what you want?

Write your answer here:

Point(s) to consider: There is no better way to build resentment in a relationship than to use sex as a tool to manipulate your partner. It poisons love and if done regularly, often leads to infidelity.

Never use your love for one another as a bargaining chip. True, it might help you get your way, but each time you use that method your partner's love for you lessens. Is what you want now really worth taking the chance of putting out the light of love in your partner's eyes?

Bottom line: If your partner wants sex, give it to them. The anger one experiences during arguments dissipates over time, but feelings of being manipulated, used and disrespected don't.

71) Do you share your concerns, fears, hopes etc?

Write your answer here:

Point(s) to consider: Once married, the two of you are in it for the long haul. And the better you know your spouse, the better your relationship will be. The 'garbage in, garbage out,' term the computer techs use also applies to relationships. Once they know what you like, love, dislike, mistrust, believe in, hope for, worry about, regret, aspire to, stand for, and will fight against, the better they can align their lives to yours, shower you with the things you love, banish the things you hate and avoid raising topics that will only lead to pointless arguments that can't be resolved.

72) Are you a free spirit or a down to earth realist?

Write your answer here:

Point(s) to consider: You've heard the saying, 'Opposite attract' and that's often true but only to a certain extent. It's advantageous to have someone who is detail-oriented when you're a big picture person, to have someone who is an extrovert when you're an introvert and for a dreamer to have someone with their feet planted firmly on the ground.

The idea is to find someone with the qualities that you lack, ***but one who also has the same basic likes and dislikes***. A deeply religious person probably won't be happy with a devout atheist. A person with an advanced education will likely be unhappy with someone with little education and an early bird will likely have trouble with a night owl.

Remember, love does not conquer all. If having that special someone in your life presents more time consuming difficulties than easing life's hardships, you're likely with the wrong person.

73) Are you dishonest?

Write your answer here:

Point(s) to consider: If you habitually lie, you're going to poison the relationship. People aren't all that complicated and over time your future mate will figure you out and once they do and discover that half of what you said wasn't true, they'll likely terminate the relationship.

So if you stopped off for a beer after work, don't say you had car trouble. And if you lost track of time on Facebook and didn't get around to doing what you should have, just admit it.

Your partner will likely be ticked but overall no harm done. Lie and get caught? That begs the question, 'What else have you lied about?'

74) Are you expectations about your spouse realistic?

Write your answer here:

Point(s) to consider: If you want misery and disappointment throughout your marriage, simply delude yourself into thinking that your future mate is that perfect someone who will be the answer to all your problems and the solution to all your concerns.

He/She won't be.

Always remember that person is only human and will, on more than one occasion, disappoint you and if that will cause your world to collapse all around you, then you had unrealistic expectations to begin with.

The key to having a happy long term relationship is to find out what their good and bad traits are and decide if you can accept them. Don't delude yourself into thinking he or she will change, or look at them as a fixer-upper. You may get them to dress better, to continue their education or stop dropping the f-bomb in every sentence, *but you're not going to change who they are.*

Everyone comes 'AS IS' and you get to 'Take it, or leave it'

Those are your options. Believing you can 'change' someone is like trying to teach a pig to dance. In the end all you've done is wasted your time and annoyed the pig.

75) Do you enjoy the same activities?

Write your answer here:

Point(s) to consider: This goes back to the 'do opposite attract' question. It's important that you both enjoy a number of the same activities so you can spend time doing them together.

And that you have similar tastes in things like music, television shows and movies. Why? Because you don't want to be in a relationship where you hate the music they listen to on the radio when you go for a Sunday drive, or the TV shows they watch when you two settle down for the evening or the movies they chose that subject you to several hours of crap you couldn't care less about.

You might really like and perhaps even love that person but a life together won't be pleasant if the two of you have such polar opposite tastes.

76) Do you fight fair?

Write your answer here:

Point(s) to consider: Well do you? You already know the answer to that one. And if you don't fight fair it's time you learned how. Don't turn on the waterworks to get your way, that's blackmail. And don't pull that 'I'm the man of the house and what I say goes' crap. Pull that and the thing that goes, will likely be <u>you</u>.

The most important thing to remember, is that in a fight between two spouses that the one who supposedly 'wins' actually loses, because the spouse that lost is now filled with resentment and is lying in wait for round two.

The most important goal in any marital spat is to find common ground in which to work out a compromise. Because 'having won.' won't fill the void created by losing the people you loved the most in divorce court.

77) Do you discuss your intimate sexual relationships with friends?

Write your answer here:

Point(s) to consider: Many TV shows show women openly discussing what they do in bed with their men with their lady friends and men doing the same with their buddies in the sports locker room after a game. It's portrayed as just something people do and should be accepted as such.

No, it shouldn't.

What a married couple does in the privacy of their bedroom is private. The marriage bed is regularly used to reveal secrets, fears, hopes and dreams to their spouse. Not a place where one has to worry about what kind of review their performance will receive at the water cooler in the morning.

Or what other intimate details are being discussed.

You keep your spouses' secrets with the same unwavering strength you would use to protect your own and never reveal them, ever.

78) If you have a bad day, do you take it out on your partner?

Write your answer here:

Point(s) to consider: If you do, **STOP**. Your future spouse should never be your personal whipping boy/girl just because life's daily problems knocked you around. Often these arguments arise when one of the partners comes home from work and the other partner immediately begins complaining about the rough day they had.

One way to avoid this is for both partners to agree not to discuss their day for one full hour after arriving home.

This gives each of you the opportunity to 'decompress' and settle into your normal routine. What follows is a discussion not a rant. There is no raising of voices or flaring of tempers.

You're together to fight the world, not each other.

79) How important is weight/appearance?

Write your answer here:

Point(s) to consider: Since this is a life-long commitment you would do well to know what your partner expects from you appearance wise. If she finds bald guys unattractive, and baldness runs in your family, you're going to need to start saving for hair-transplants.

And if it's important to him that you maintain that firm and fit body you presently have, then prepare to be spending time at the gym.

And tell your partner these things now. We are what we are, and we like what we like. Neither of you is likely to change so knowing what may be potential problems will give you the time you'll need to prepare.

80) Hobbies, how much time gets reserved for it?

Write your answer here:

Point(s) to consider: Overall, hobbies are good for you. They release stress, increase brain capacity and improve dexterity. However sometimes they can become an obsession and a way to avoid more serious problems.

One of the divorced men I interviewed said that his wife's knitting hobby grew into an obsession as the marriage deteriorated. She'd knit watching television, while riding in the car and even on the toilet. But she never actually created anything other than large blankets and very long scarves.

Men too, use hobbies for the same reason, usually working in the garage or the basement on projects that never seem to end.

Always remember that they are only hobbies. Fun things you enjoy doing to pass the time. They are not lifestyles. Your home shouldn't become a display department for your collection of rare and unusual toasters for example.

If it has, the time has come to turn that hobby into a business and move it out of your home. Homes are for families, businesses belong in warehouses and storefronts.

81) Personal hygiene. Do you expect your spouse to take a shower every day?

Write your answer here:

Point(s) to consider: Make it very clear how you feel about personal hygiene to your future partner and make sure you both agree on what's expected from the other. There are no hard and fast rules here other than setting mutually agreeable expectations and sticking to them. If she likes the three day scruffy beard look, fine, if not, start shaving every day. If he doesn't mind some hair on her legs, again fine, if he does then she needs to shave every day too.

Same rules apply to pubic hair. Make sure your genital area is as esthetically pleasing to your mate as possible. Remember, they're the person you want to turn on and looking and smelling as pleasing as possible is the best way to accomplish that.

Also see that your hair, finger nails and toe nails are kept clean and cut to an acceptable size. Any discoloration or odd growth of the nails should be seen to by a professional.

82) Have you or spouse ever had a sexually transmitted disease?

Write your answer here:

Point(s) to consider: You should inform your future spouse of any viral sexually transmitted disease you've contracted and had treated such as Genital Herpes, HIV, Hepatitis B and HPV.

Virus's can lay dormant for lengthy periods and then flare up without notice. They are also transmittable in their dormant phase.

These can be life changing should they be contracted and your partner should be made fully aware of the risk.

83) Have you ever had a possibly reoccurring disease?

Write your answer here:

Point(s) to consider: If you've had a serious illness that can possibly return like cancer or malaria, it is important to inform your future spouse of the possibility. They should be made aware of any and all factors regarding your health so he/she can make informed decisions as to whether they want to assume the responsibility of caring for you while you're undergoing treatment and perhaps even dealing with losing you should the treatment be unsuccessful.

You future mate may have many sterling qualities but don't assume care-giver is one of them. If the illness does return you don't want the added pressure of him/her abandoning you during such a difficult time.

84) What is your future spouse's past? Does he/she have an ex-spouse? Children? Child support payments?

Write your answer here:

Point(s) to consider: This may a lot more important than you realize. If you marry someone paying child support, depending on the state, your income may be considered part of his income and the support payment amount may increase. In addition, should you divorce, you may still be required to continue paying into that child's support even though you aren't genetically related to them as the courts often feel it is unfair to penalize the child should a marriage end.

Another important issue is whether your future spouse is paying alimony and how much. Like the spouse with the large credit card debt mentioned earlier, most of your future partners income will be redirected to pay those court ordered responsibilities.

The best way to handle this is to contact a lawyer practicing family law. Knowing the possible financial pitfalls may affect your decision to continue your relationship.

85) If of different religions, are all your religious practices acceptable to your spouse?

Write your answer here:

Point(s) to consider: As civilization become more globalized it's important to know what type of background your future spouse comes from and what rituals and ceremonies his/her religion practices. Some have very strict and stern demands regarding diet, behavior and dress. Others rigorous prayer rituals, other still require the sacrificing of animals.

Some religious rituals and ceremonies are abhorrent to people not originally from that culture and they will quickly end any relationship with the person who practices it.

If you are not aware of the requirements of your future spouses' religion or culture, become aware and learn all you need to know before committing to marrying them.

86) Is masturbation acceptable after marriage?

Write your answer here:

Point(s) to consider: The two of you need to agree on this because if you don't the moment one leaves the house the other will get right down to business. And should that partner be caught, there will be a big argument, promises made and the practice will likely continue only this time they'll be more careful.

If your partner enjoys masturbating there is nothing you can do about it, other than force them to do it behind your back and then lie.

That's a lousy way to run a trusted relationship.

87) How do you feel about pornography?

Write your answer here:

Point(s) to consider: If ever an answer was more routinely lied about than this one I don't what it is. The feelings about porn vary. Some couples enjoy it and say it adds spice to their marriage. Others considered it degrading toward woman and leads to infidelity. Whatever your views on porn, you should hash them out before marriage because nowadays even in widely distributed commercial movies there are instances of graphic sex and nudity.

88) Bi-sexuality. Have you ever had sex with a person of your own gender?

Write your answer here:

Point(s) to consider: It is absolute essential that your partner is fully aware of your sexual needs and desires. If you tried it and decided that it wasn't something you wanted to experience again then leave it in the past. On the other hand if it is something that excites you then your future spouse needs to know.

And they have to decide if it matters to them.

As stated in the very beginning 'Every marriage makes its own rules' and if they don't care then it doesn't matter. If they do care then you'd better hash it out now, and decide how it will be handled.

89) Would you consider it cheating if your spouse had sex with someone of their own gender while you were married?

Write your answer here:

Point(s) to consider: Whatever you decide here is something you will likely have to stick with. To some spouses that's a turn on and have no trouble with it. With others it's a fast track to divorce court.

Whatever you decide regarding this practice by your mate make sure YOU decide it. Don't be influenced by what society or friends or family might think about it. It's none of their business.

Just remember, once a third person is brought into the mix,

emotions like jealousy, envy and resentment may start factoring in.

90) What are you views regarding mate swapping/threesomes/open marriage?

Write your answer here:

Point(s) to consider: This is another instance where your marriage makes its own rules. I know a couple who were very much into the swinging lifestyle and are still happily married after forty years. For other couples, wanting to swing is often an indication that the marriage is in trouble or coming to a close.

Do not assume your partner thinks the same way you do when it comes to sex. Often people who think alike on many issues are stunned when they learn their partner has very different views regarding sexual activity.

Also do not assume the partner is dissatisfied with you physically or sexually. They may be an adrenaline junkie or free spirit, neither of which has anything to do with you.

Again, bringing other people into the sexual mix often leads to more problems than it solves, because things seen cannot be unseen and things done cannot be undone, should the sexual experiment turn out badly.

Bottom line. Know what you're getting into and accept the outcome.

91) How would you respond if you discovered your spouse was a cross dresser?

Write your answer here:

Point(s) to consider: Because a person cross dresses does not automatically make them a homosexual. It often has more to do with how they feel about themselves and what they need to do to in order feel good about themselves. It will not likely affect your sexual relationship nor their feelings for you.

Basically it's simply something they do. And like masturbation, if you frown upon it, they are going to do it anyway when you're not around.

Now is the time to make your feelings known and to consider how this practice will be addressed once children enter the mix.

92) How important is marital fidelity to you and your future spouse?

Write your answer here:

Point(s) to consider: If one spouse demands complete fidelity and the other doesn't there is going to be problems. Some people can separate love from sex and others can't. Some feel sex is a fun activity to be had whenever and with whoever happens to be willing. Others view infidelity as the worst form of betrayal.

You love each other and would never want to hurt your partner so now is the time to sort out your feelings on this. There will likely be children down the road and the choices you make now will affect them too.

Make sure you both agree to and fully understand the marriage rule you make here, it will factor into your relationship for the rest of your married life.

93) How often do you desire sex in any given week?

Write your answer here:

Point(s) to consider: In this case don't assume anything. Just because society has us believe the woman doesn't need as much sex as the man, doesn't make it true. Nor should you assume that because he's a man he'll be willing to have sex anytime you want it.

Sexual needs are generated by hormones and personal desires and each person is different. That sweet fresh-faced innocent looking Pollyanna may be a sexual animal and require it at least once a day. And that muscular, masculine, hard-bodied stud may only be in the mood once every two weeks.

You are both going to be VERY disappointed if your needs aren't relatively similar to each others. What is seen as excessive demands to one may be viewed as frigidity by the other, so make sure you give full disclosure on this.

There is nothing wrong regarding how big or how little one's sexual appetite is, just make sure you're both in the same ballpark or there will be problems down the road.

94) Do you enjoy oral sex?

Write your answer here:

Point(s) to consider: If you enjoy giving and receiving it and there are no concerns regarding STD's then there is no problem. If on the other hand your partner recoils from performing the act then you need to address that now.

Be upfront with your feelings regarding this. If you don't like doing it or find the act off-putting, you partner needs to know. No one should be obligated to do something in bed they find unpleasant, however, if a specific act is to be removed from the sexual menu, your partner should be made aware.

I once heard a woman say as she was exiting her bachelorette party, "I know it really turns him on when I give him a (oral sex) but I don't like it one bit and after we get married I'm putting an end to that once and for all.

Remember what I said about resentment?

95) Would you agree to anal sex?

Write your answer here:

Point(s) to consider: This usually comes up a few times during marriage especially if the couple is looking to spice things up. Since it's usually the woman on the receiving end, she gets final says on if, how and when it is, or isn't, done.

Because of its usual function, health concerns should be discussed and agreed upon before any act regarding that area is initiated.

96) Would you be open to sexual experimentation? (Sex toys, bondage, spanking etc)

Write your answer here:

Point(s) to consider: This question usually comes up after years of marriage and both partners are looking for something new to try. Most times it's harmless and can often revitalize a love life that's fallen into routine.

But make sure your partner doesn't have any strong objections to this. Once again don't assume that your future spouse's sexual turn-ons are the same as yours. They may view such activities as perverse and degenerate.

Sexual desires sometimes change as we age and we may be more open to new experiences but if your partner is dead set against it, either accept it or consider jumping back into the dating pool.

97) What are your views about dangerous activities? (Driving a motorcycle, sky-diving, bungee jumping)

Write your answer here:

Point(s) to consider: Some people are adrenaline junkies and live for the thrill of adventure and danger. They bungee jump, zip-line, skydive and run with the bulls, for that rush. Exciting activities are fun and best done while you are still young and your strength and reflexes are at their peak.

But once children come along those activities need to be put away. Lose an eye, leg, arm, foot and suffer brain damage because you felt you could take the adventure just one step farther is selfish and highly detrimental to your family.

One of the realities of marriage is that you are no longer living for just yourself anymore, you are living for your family and need to keep doing so. But take heart, you can always go back to being Danger Dan/Danielle once the kids are out on their own.

98) What are your views on unhealthy activities? (Smoking, drinking, gambling, recreational drug use.)

Write your answer here:

Point(s) to consider: What's that old saying "Everything in moderation?" Well that's true but with marriage comes the time to start thinking about the long haul and the big picture. With a pack of cigarettes and a six pack of beer hovering around ten dollars apiece, a lot of money could be set aside for the purchases of far better things if those unhealthy activities were kicked to the curb.

On the other hand everybody needs to cut loose now and then so keep the 'Everything in moderation' adage in mind when you consider both your bad habits as well as your need for frugality and self sacrifice

99) What is the one thing about your future spouse that annoys you the most?

Write your answer here:

Point(s) to consider: Although what you have to say may hurt their feelings, it must be done. As stated in the beginning of this book, resentment kills marriages.

And how sad would it be if one partner –instead of making their problem known— suffered in silence until that resentment grew to the point where they started hating their spouse? And the spouse had no idea why.

Marriage ain't for sissies. There will be times when very serious problems will have to be faced and hard decisions made. So if your future spouse can't handle constructive criticism and reacts by becoming emotionally hysterical or explosively angry when you tell them what they do that annoys you, then they are living in a world of unreasonable expectations and need to spent some more time in the minor leagues before stepping up to the Big Game.

Adults solve problems, children place blame.

100) How do you feel about your spouse starting their own business?

Write your answer here:

Point(s) to consider: Because the economy has been so shaky for so long, more people are considering striking out on their own and starting their own companies.

It takes time for business's to grow and often requires you and your spouse taking out loans and using all your assets for collateral. On average seven out of ten business's fail within the first few years primarily because they didn't have enough capital to weather the business building process.

This is a high risk, big benefit decision. And one where there's no changing one's mind once started. The danger here is that your spouse may resent you for not supporting them when they wanted to start their own business and the possibility equal resentment on the opposite side when you convince your spouse to support your choice and the business crashes and winds up costing the both of you all of your assets as well as your house.

Again this is one of those instances where an agreed upon decision must be made before starting out and an acceptance of how things turn out whether successful or not.

The Happily Ever After

In conclusion, the most important marriage rules are the ones that, when obeyed, make you and your spouse's life better and your marriage stronger.

And men and women have certain differences, accept that. Because no matter how hard you try, you're not going to change what's genetically ingrained, so pay attention here and you'll avoid many an argument.

For example:

> **Women are subtle, Men aren't. Women like to allude to things, Men don't get hints, period.** If you want something, or want your man to know something, don't hint at it, tell them exactly what it is you want. It may not be romantic but you won't be disappointed when your man gets it right the first time.

Women like to talk about their problems and when they do they want their man to listen, not attempt to fix it. If she wants you to fix it she'll say so.

Don't EVER buy a woman a household appliance as a gift.

Women like to chat, Men don't. When women get chatty men tune them out. Women are curious, men aren't. Women want to know details. Men figure if that person wanted the details known they would have spoken up.

Women like romance, men don't. If a man is being attentive, romantic and saying all the right things, he's not interested in getting into a relationship, he's interested in getting her into bed.

Women need to be reassured that they are sexually attractive.
NEVER poke fun at a woman's appearance. Men may think they're being funny but women view it as abusive and hateful.

Never deflate a man's ego.
Sometimes that's all he has left.

Pay special attention to how they treat service people. People who are short tempered and abusive to people in low level job are bullies. Anyone working at making an honest living should be treated with respect.

Notice how they treat animals.
Your future spouse doesn't have to love animals. Some people are just too busy but if he/she is purposefully cruel or threatening toward a defenseless creature, take it as a warning sign.

There are many others, but you'll pick up on them as time goes by.

Regardless to what marriage rules you add to your relationship, the following are the five most important and should included at the top of every married couple's list.

1) The welfare and happiness of your spouse comes before all else.

2) Never leave them without saying I love you. One day they will likely be your last words to them.

3) Never offer your spouse's services without consulting with them first.

4) Never discuss what you do in bed with anyone other than your spouse

5) Always take your spouse's side in any disagreement, even if they're wrong.

One last thing: No marriage is perfect and no person is perfect. And every marriage makes its own rules. And the most important thing to remember that once those rules are created and agreed upon, they can only be changed through mutual agreement otherwise they must never be broken. Because marriage is trust. You will be trusting your future spouse with your emotional well-being, with your money, with your health, with your business and with the raising of your children. And with that being said I am going to ask you both to answer one last bonus question.

101) How would you feel if your future spouse had instead been your parent when you were a child and had raised you?
Write you answer here:

Point(s) to consider: If you shudder at the thought of that moody bad-boy being your father or that self-centered flirt being your mother then consider what you're subjecting your future children to.

You might find them exciting or challenging but if they clearly aren't parental material then you need to ask yourself just why are you marrying them?

So that's it my friends. I hope this questionnaire helped you see what your future spouse is truly like and that they're even better than you expected.

May you both have a long and happy life together.

www.ingramcontent.com/pod-product-compliance
Lightning Source LLC
Chambersburg PA
CBHW071003040426
42443CB00007B/637